WILLIAM BYRD

Eight Fragmentary Songs

from Edward Paston's Lute-Book, British Library Add. MS 31992
edited and reconstructed by Andrew Johnstone

CONTENTS

Sources and Abbreviations ii
Preface ii
    Byrd's Fragmentary Songs ii
    Paston's Lutebooks and the Spanish Vihuela Tradition iii
    Clefs, Lute Tunings and Content Order iv
    Method of Reconstructing Instrumental and Vocal Parts vii
    The Poetry ix
    The Authority and Use of the Reconstructions xi
    A Note on Performing Pitch xii
    Acknowledgements xii
Editorial Method xiii
Textual Commentary xiii

Songs for solo voice and four instruments

1   Ah, youthful years 1
2   In tower most high 6
3   Lo, dead he lives *to the music of* What wights are these? 9
4   Narcissus lov'd *to the music of* With sighs and tears 13
5   What grieves my bones? *to the music of* O happy thrice 16

Songs for solo voice, or duet, and four instruments with chorus

6   Depart, ye furies 20
7   I will give laud 26
8   Look and bow down 29

Parts available direct from the publisher.

Fretwork Publishing
16 Teddington Park Road, Teddington, Middx TW11 8ND, UK
+44 (0)208 977 0924   +44 (0)7717 474263
info@fretworkpublishing.co.uk
www.fretworkpublishing.co.uk

© 2020 Fretwork Editions, London. General Editors: Bill Hurt & Julia Hodgson
ISBN 978-1-8382144-0-1   ISMN 979-0-708099-14-7

SOURCES AND ABBREVIATIONS

423	John Petre's partbook: Oxford, Bodleian Library, MS Mus. Sch. e. 423
1588	*Psalmes, sonets, & songs of sadnes and pietie ... by William Byrd* (London: Thomas East, 1588; STC 4253)
1589	*Songs of sundrie natures ... By VVilliam Byrd* (London: Thomas East, 1589; STC 4256)
1611	*Psalmes, songs and sonnets ... by William Byrd* (London: Thomas Snodham; STC 4255)
BE	The Byrd Edition, gen. ed. Philip Brett, 17 vols (London: Stainer & Bell, 1970–2004)
CE	*A choice of emblemes, and other deuises, for the moste parte gathered out of sundrie writers, Englished and moralized. And diuers newly deuised, by Geffrey Whitney* (Leyden: Francis Raphelengius, 1586; STC 25438)
CMC	*The countrie mans comfort. Or Religious recreations fitte for all well disposed persons. Which was printed in the yeere of our Lord 1588. And since corrected, amended, and enlarged by the same author. I. R.* (London: M. Dawson, 1637; STC 20961)
PDD	*The paradyse of daynty deuises* (London: Henry Disle, 1576; STC 7516) and later edns
PL	Edward Paston's lutebook: London, British Library, Add. MS 31992
S&H	Thomas Sternhold, John Hopkins, et al, *The whole booke of Psalmes collected into Englysh metre* (London: John Day, 1562 etc.; STC 2430, 2432 et seq.)
SNG/4	Text of 'Look and bow down': Greenwich, Royal Maritime Museum, MS SNG/4 (formerly MS FD/2)
TM	'Tottell's miscellany': *Songes and sonettes written by the right honorable Lorde Henry Howard late Earle of Surrey, and others*, 2nd edn (London: Richardum Tottell, 1557; STC 13862)

Works from Byrd's own publications are identified by year and sequence number (e.g. 1588/1); his MS works are identified by BE volume and sequence number (e.g. BE15/2)

PREFACE

Byrd's Fragmentary Songs

Byrd's enthusiasm for publishing his own music, though amply witnessed by some 200 Latin-texted works and between seventy and eighty original vocal partsongs,[1] never fully extended to his nearly one hundred strophic settings for vocal solo or duet with four (or occasionally five) accompanying instruments assumed—though this is nowhere stated in the sources—to have been viols. While between forty and fifty of these works—now universally known, albeit ahistorically, as 'consort songs'[2]—did find their way into Byrd's publications, a mere six appear there in their original instrumental format (1589/35, 40 and 41; 1611/28, 31 and 32), the composer having adapted the remainder into vocal partsongs.[3] Seemingly there did not yet exist the market for instrumentally accompanied vocal music that would eventually be supplied by Byrd's younger contemporaries John Amner, Martin Peerson and especially Michael East.

Thus, of the genres in which Byrd published, it is the so-called consort songs that comprise by far the highest proportion of unpublished items. Their survival in MS is due chiefly to the avid collecting instincts of the noted amateur lutenist Edward Paston (1550–1630), a friend of the composer and a fellow Catholic, who amassed not only numerous partbook sets but also what are mentioned in his will as 'many lutebooks pricked in ciphers',[4] five of which are known still to be extant. Of these, British Library Add. MS 31992 (hereinafter PL) contains the greatest number of Byrd's consort songs (more items by him, indeed, than any other MS), and seems intended as a lutenist's compendium—in the inalienably abbreviated medium of tablature—of all the songs Byrd had composed by c.1600.[5] It contains all eight songs here reconstructed, and is the sole source for the music of seven of them, the eighth having a single musical concordance in Bodleian MS Mus. Sch. e. 423 (hereinafter 423), an

---

1 These approximate figures are based on the numbering system of Byrd's publications, where each *pars* of a composition in two or more *partes* is reckoned as a separate item. The exact number of published original partsongs cannot be determined because items in that category are not always easily differentiated from adapted consort songs. To be sure, in his 1588 songbook Byrd in most cases labelled the original solo voice of adapted consort songs as 'the first singing part'. Yet in claiming that *all* the 1588 songs are adaptations, Kerman repudiated the absence of that designation from six items (nos 1, 17, 18, 20, 21 and 24), only one of which (no. 24) exists also in a MS consort version. Nor indeed do the openings of three of those six (nos 1, 18 and 21) introduce the voices in the manner of a consort song, where 'the first singing part' is the last to enter. In the 1589 songbook, moreover, no items have a designated 'first singing part', even though three (nos 29, 31 and 32) exist in MS consort versions (BE16/29–31). On this (still open) question, see Kerman, *The Elizabethan Madrigal: A Comparative Study* (New York: American Musicological Society, 1962), 102–6; BE12, p. viii; BE13, p. xii; Jeremy Smith, *Verse and Voice in Byrd's Song Collections of 1588 and 1589* (Woodbridge: Boydell Press, 2016), 7–9.

2 The term itself is historical, but its application to the genre in question is due to Philip Brett: see his 'The English Consort Song, 1570–1625', *Proceedings of the Royal Musical Association*, 88 (1961–2), 73–88 (73).

3 The exact number of published adapted consort songs cannot be determined for the reasons given in n. 1 above.

4 Quoted in Brett, 'Edward Paston (1550–1630): A Norfolk Gentleman and His Musical Collection', *Transactions of the Cambridge Bibliographical Society*, 4 (1964), 51–69 (66).

5 Brett, 'Edward Paston', 65–6, 69, 'Pitch and Transposition in the Paston Manuscripts' in *Sundry Sorts of Music Books: Essays on the British Library Collections: Presented to O. W. Neighbour on His 70th Birthday*, edited by Chris Banks, Arthur Searle, and Malcolm Turner (London: British Library, 1993), 89–118 (92).

orphaned contratenor partbook copied for the Catholic aristocrat and Byrd-patron John Petre.[6]

Owing to losses from Paston's collection over time,[7] some twenty of Byrd's known consort songs are now lacking one or more of their vocal and/or instrumental parts. Ten of these were included among the forty-one authenticated MS songs of BE15, and incorporate material reconstructed by the editor Philip Brett. Four of Brett's ten reconstructions were lacking single instrumental parts (BE15/2, 20, 23 and 24) and a further four the solo vocal part (BE15/3, 5, 21 and 27). Nor was Brett deterred by two, more seriously eroded songs. In the case of 'O God, but God' (BE15/6), which retains only one of its four instrumental parts, the missing material could be derived from two contemporary arrangements for lute and another for keyboard. Similarly in the case of 'Truce for a time' (BE15/25), which retains only its vocal part, one of Paston's lute arrangements aided the reconstitution of the three lowest parts, leaving only the topmost instrumental part to be editorially recomposed.

Brett appears very nearly to have succeeded in reconstructing 'Look and bow down' (8), and might well have done so had he inferred that each of the song's three verses was scored differently from the others (see p. x below). But this lute arrangement, together with the others reconstructed here, remained in Brett's opinion 'beyond reclaim'.[8] Edmund Fellowes had likewise deemed the same arrangements 'too fragmentary to suggest the possibility of reconstruction', and in his own edition had given only their incipits in quasi polyphonic two-stave realisations.[9] For BE, Brett adopted the same format, shortening the incipits given by Fellowes. Presumably the intention of both editors was to help others identify any vocal or instrumental MS concordances that might eventually re-emerge: to date, however, none has.

Work on the present collection has enabled all fifteen song fragments that were not reconstructed for BE confidently to be categorised as either consort songs or partsongs. Two items known only from their two uppermost parts (BE16/39 and 43) are self-evidently consort songs (my reconstructions of which are to be published separately), while the two voice parts that constitute the remains of 'Preces Deo fundamus' (BE16/44) clearly show it to have been a partsong.[10] PL additionally transmits four Byrdian *unica* (v. 2 of BE15/23, BE16/35, 36 and 46) that are identifiable as partsongs chiefly because they exhibit too few of the characteristics that, as we shall see, make reconstruction of the consort songs feasible. Whether or not those four partsongs also will prove capable of reconstruction remains to be seen.

Paston's Lutebooks and the Spanish Vihuela Tradition
In terms both of their form of tablature (numeric as opposed to literal) and their content (arrangements of polyphony as opposed to original lute music), Paston's lutebooks are rooted in vihuela methods he is presumed to have assimilated as a young man during much time spent in Spain.[11] Since most of PL's contents still exist also in their native polyphonic formats, the arrangements can be seen to represent the originals in great detail. The formidable demands they place on the player's skill suggest there may have been more than mere flattery in Geoffrey Whitney's emblem *Orphei musica*, of which the mysterious dedicatee 'D. St. Bullum' was clearly one of Paston's neighbours:

E. P. Esquire [in margin]
But, you are happy most,
    who in such place do stay;
You need not Thracia seek,
    to hear some imp of Orpheus play,
Since, that so near your home,
    Apollo's darling dwells;
Who Linus, and Amphion stains,
    and Orpheus far excels.[12]

Two factors suggest the arrangements are the work of Paston himself, or at least that they were prepared under his close supervision. First, although the lutebooks were copied by a professional scribe identifiable as one of his servants,[13] a single item in PL has been shown to be in Paston's own hand (ff. 54v–55r).[14] Second, as Hector Sequera has demonstrated, the arrangements embody vihuela practice in a manner otherwise unknown in England, especially with regard to tuning and fingering.[15] Since the second factor has a direct bearing on the method of reconstructing the PL *unica*, it calls for some explanation.

The question of lute tuning is conveniently illustrated by the item from PL just referred to, an arrangement 'alio modo' of Byrd's unpublished partsong 'What vaileth it to rule?' (BE16/6). Possibly made for one of Paston's sons to play, it was clearly intended as a more practicable alternative to another arrangement of the same song entered earlier in the MS and incorporating all five original voice parts (f. 49, the folio containing bb. 1–44 is now missing). Not only does the alternative arrangement omit the two highest voice parts (presumably to convert the partsong into a vocal duet), but also it is intabulated for a lute in E tuning as opposed to the G tuning used for the first, five-part arrangement. Albeit cautiously, Brett assumed all Paston's lute tablatures to represent G tuning,[16] and misleadingly described the alternative arrangement as 'transposed' and 'up a minor third'.[17] In fact, this item shows that Paston, following precisely a method described

---

6 On this MS see David Mateer, 'William Byrd, John Petre and Oxford, Bodleian MS Mus. Sch. e. 423', *Royal Musical Association Research Chronicle*, 29 (1996), 21–46.
7 Probably the most catastrophic losses occurred when Paston's old house at the now abandoned Norfolk village of Appleton was destroyed by fire in 1707; the fire is mentioned in Charles Parkin, An *Essay Towards a Topographical History of the County of Norfolk*, vol. 8, 2nd edn (London: William Miller, 1808), 330.
8 BE15, p. viii.
9 THE COLLECTED VOCAL WORKS OF WILLIAM BYRD, vol. 16 (London: Stainer & Bell, 1948), pp. [vi], 151–3.

10 See Fellowes, *William Byrd*, 2nd edn (London: Oxford University Press, 1948), 167–9.
11 Hector Sequera, 'House Music for Recusants in Elizabethan England: Performance Practice in the Music Collection of Edward Paston (1550–1630)' (PhD diss., University of Birmingham, 2010), 1, 16–19.
12 CE, 186.
13 Brett, 'Edward Paston', 58.
14 Brett, 'Pitch and Transposition', 98.
15 'House Music for Recusants', 92–4.
16 'Pitch and Transposition', 96.
17 BE16, p. 189; 'Pitch and Transposition', 98.

in Juan Bermudo's *Declaración de instrumentos musicales* of 1555, had arrived at the simplest possible fingering by considering the various possibilities yielded by a range of different lute tunings.[18] (It may be noted that such changes in tuning do not involve scordatura but affect all six courses equally, the middle pair remaining tuned a major third apart and the remainder in perfect fourths.)

The PL arrangements further observe the vihuela tradition in that most of them omit the topmost part, this having remained in staff notation for performance by a solo voice or, as we shall see, possibly an instrument.[19] A companion partbook to PL, with contents in the same order, indubitably formed part of Paston's collection, for the folio number of each item it contained appears at the head of the corresponding item in PL itself, in the hand of the main scribe. That partbook was almost certainly one of several described in Paston's will as 'singing p[ar]ts … w[hi]ch must be sung to the lute' and which were 'tied up with the lute parts'.[20] No further sightings of it, however, have ever been reported. Had it survived, the Byrdian *unica* whose topmost parts it contained would doubtless already have been reconstructed by modern scholars.

This aspect of the vihuela method lent itself straightforwardly to those consort songs in which the solo vocal part was topmost. In such cases, the resulting arrangement resembles regular lute-song format, albeit with a lute part of considerably above-average density and difficulty. Yet in a substantial minority of Byrd's consort songs the solo vocal part is of course the second part from the top, the topmost instead forming an instrumental descant. In such cases, the descant being too high for the lute, the solo vocal part was instead included in the intabulation and the descant assigned to the companion partbook. (It is uncertain whether the descants were played on an instrument or were indeed 'sung to the lute', leaving the actual vocal part unsung; but this question is irrelevant to the reconstruction method.)

PL and its lost companion were connected by yet another observance of vihuela custom. As in certain printed anthologies of motets and canciones arranged for vihuela and voice,[21] Paston's scribe indicated, at the head of each lute intabulation and in Spanish, the course number (from highest sounding to lowest sounding) and fret number (vice versa) that equate to the first note of the topmost part. Thus, for example, at the head of 'Ah, youthful years' (**1**) there appears the rubric 'La p[rimera] all 3. t[raste]' (the first course, the third fret). Elsewhere, these rubrics have been interpreted as directions for the lutenist to sound the singer's first note before embarking on the song,[22] yet it is equally possible that the lutenist was instead expected to refer to the first note of the topmost part and tune the instrument accordingly. As we shall see (p. x), the Spanish rubric of **8** applies to the first note of stanza two, which a singer would hardly have benefited from hearing before stanza one.

Clefs, Lute Tunings and Content Order
As Brett first pointed out,[23] the contents of PL (and, by inference, the contents also of its lost companion partbook) show purely musical signs of systematic organisation. Brett's observation that this organisation 'involved clef combinations' (p. 93) is certainly borne out by the surviving original polyphony, yet seems at odds with the simple circumstance that PL, being in tablature, itself contains not a single clef. The organisation makes sense, however, first if each clef combination is understood to be conducive to one or more particular lute tunings, and secondly if the companion partbook is seen to have been divided into sections respectively containing solo vocal parts and instrumental descants.

The clef combinations employed in Byrd's consort songs are many and various, but may be clearly divided into the three categories shown in ex. 1. For present purposes, these categories will be differentiated by their usual outermost clefs: F4–G2, F3–G2 and F4–C1. It should be noted, however, that in combination (b) the lowest clef is occasionally C4 instead of F3, and that in combination (c) the use of the C2 clef instead of the C1 clef for the topmost voice seldom if ever symptomises any difference in the vocal range.

With a maximum range of twenty-three notes, the F4–G2 combination is with a few notable exceptions reserved for those

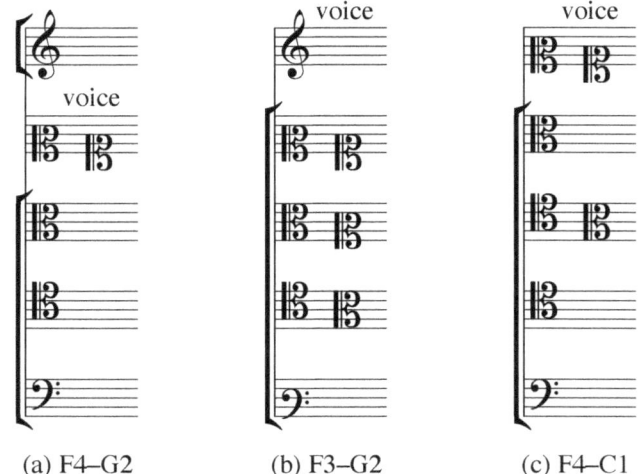

(a) F4–G2   (b) F3–G2   (c) F4–C1

Ex. 1. Cleffing of Byrd's consort songs

songs with a topmost instrumental part, the description 'great compass' being applied by Byrd himself to the vocal ensemble arrangements of such items printed in his 1588 songbook. The F3–G2 and F4–C1 combinations between them cover the same written range as the F4–G2 combination, yet all those 1588 songs in which they are deployed are described in Byrd's preface as 'fit for the reach of most voices', an assertion that makes sense only if the F3–G2 items and the F4–C1 items are brought into closer alignment by some degree of transposition.

In sixteenth-century vocal polyphony generally, it is by no means unusual for a given composition to be cleffed F3–G2 in one source and F4–C1 in another, the latter source being a fourth (or, less often, a fifth) lower than the former.[24] Byrd's *œuvre* is no exception: for example, seven items from his printed songbooks (1588/1, 10, 18, 19 and 28 and 1591/30 and 33) were copied a fourth or a fifth higher and in different clefs in Paston's partbooks, British Library Add. MSS 29401–5.[25] It is true that

---

18   Sequera, 'House Music for Recusants', 75–9.
19   On the possibility that Paston's arrangements were used as 'sol-faing songs', see Stewart McCoy, 'Edward Paston and the Textless Lute-Song', *Early Music*, 15 (1987), 221–7.
20   Quoted in Brett, 'Edward Paston', 67.
21   Sequera, 'House Music for Recusants', 69–70, 80, 93–4.
22   Brett, 'Edward Paston', 57, and 'Pitch and Transposition', 96.
23   'Pitch and Transposition', 92–8.
24   On this much discussed subject see Patrizio Barbieri, 'Chiavette and Modal Transposition in Italian Practice (*c*.1500–1837)', *Recercare*, 3 (1991), 5–79, and my article '"High" Clefs in Composition and Performance', *Early Music*, 34 (2006), 29–53.

not all scholars have embraced the principle that pieces in the 'high' clefs F3–G2 should always be performed a fourth lower than they are notated.[26] Yet (to take a compelling example) when that principle is applied to Byrd's three Latin mass ordinaries, which are cleffed in various forms of the F3–G2 combination,[27] the resulting voice ranges correspond precisely with those of his vernacular Great Service, cleffed F4–C1.[28] Possibly this was why, in the first printing of the 1588 songbook, the topmost parts of the first two F4–G2 items (nos 3–4) are labelled 'triplex', whereas none of the topmost parts of the F3–G2 items is so labelled. The label may therefore have been intended to warn performers against mistaking the topmost clef of the F4–G2 combination as a signal to transpose down a fourth.[29]

If fourth-lower clef transposition is assumed to have been a principle in the organisation of PL, then the first seventy-three items in the MS fall into three layers, each defined by a common lute tuning:[30]

1–33	E
34–66	G
67–73	F

The surviving concordances show a majority of the first thirty-three items to have been cleffed F3–G2 (as too were five additional items originally entered between nos 26 and 27 on folios that are now missing).[31] A sub-group of five (nos 9–13) are instead cleffed F4–C1, but the lute tuning is unaffected by this.[32] Of the next forty items, nos 34–56 are cleffed F4–G2 and nos 57–73 F4–C1. Whereas nos 37–56 adopt the usual 'great compass' format with instrumental descant, a distinct initial sub-group is formed by nos 34–6, shown by its first item, 'La virginella' (1588/24), to have been songs unusually scored with a topmost solo triplex voice.[33]

A fourth layer comprises mixed tunings:

74	G	'Compell the hawk' (1589/28)
75	F/G?	'Behold how good' (*unicum* with final G or A)
76	[G]	'While that a cruel fire' (*unicum* with final G)
77	G	'Delight is dead' (BE15/30)
78	[G]	'Look and bow down' (**8**, *unicum* with final G)
79	F	'Christ rising' (1589/46–7)

The tunings of nos 74, 77 and 79 are indicated by concordances, while nos 76 and 78 must be for lute in G because (a) lutes in E and F would place the music in the anachronistic keys of E minor and F minor, and (b) a lute in A is nowhere else called for in the MS. In this layer, the organisation is based not on tuning but on the items' original scoring, for all are either consort duets or partsongs with two medius parts (as too were three further items originally entered directly after no. 79 on folios that are now missing).[34]

From this point, items appear to have been added to PL more haphazardly and as afterthoughts to the main corpus. Songs attributed to Parsons and Strogers, together with various anonymous items, are mingled with a few remaining Byrdiana, most of them *opera dubia*. No. 82, Byrd's church anthem 'How long shall mine enemies', is misattributed to Tallis. No. 95, the alternative arrangement of 'What vaileth it to rule?' mentioned above, ends this portion of the MS, the remaining contents being arrangements of fifty-four motets by composers (mostly continental) other than Byrd. Notwithstanding the evident disintegration of order towards the end of the Byrdian portion, it will be clear from the foregoing that the first seventy-nine items in PL's lost companion partbook were layered thus:

1–33	solo vocal parts (medius)
34–6	solo vocal parts (triplex)
37–56	instrumental descants
57–73	solo vocal parts (medius)
74–9	vocal parts from duets (or paired medius)

On the basis of PL's organisation, the following firm conclusions may be drawn about the eight *unica* here reconstructed:

1, **2** and **5** (PL nos 14, 17 and 19) lie safely within the layer of F3–G2 pieces arranged for lute in E to sound a fourth lower than their staff notation, and represent the beginning, middle and end of a sub-group of pieces with final C (nos 14–19). So definite is this evidence that it must be allowed to controvert the notation of the single surviving instrumental part for **5**, which—for reasons upon which it is unnecessary to speculate here—is given in 423 with a signature of two flats, a tone lower than the other pieces in the sub-group. Were the 423 part to represent the correct transposition, then the arrangement would be the only one for lute in G among nos 1–33 of PL, and the tessitura of the reconstructed vocal part would be unusually high. **4** (PL no 30) also lies safely within the F3–G2 layer, and belongs to a sub-group of pieces with written final A (nos 29–32).

3 (PL no 52) appears towards the end of the F4–G2 layer for lute in G. It is immediately followed by 'If that a sinner's sighs' (1588/30=BE16/23), a song with which it shares a common final (D) and certain thematic material (both songs culminate in passages of *fuga* based on strikingly similar subjects). **7** (PL

---

25 On transposed concordances of Byrd's Latin works, see my article 'The Performing Pitch of William Byrd's Latin Liturgical Polyphony: A Guide for Historically Minded Interpreters', *REA: A Journal of Religion, Education and the Arts*, 10 (2016), 79–107 (90–91).
26 Sequera, for example, in his detailed study of the practical use of Paston's music collection, has followed Brett and others in presuming performance at written pitch, whatever the clef combination ('House Music for Recusants', 100–101).
27 The Masses are respectively cleffed C4 C3 C2 (omitting a topmost G2 part), C4 C3 C2 G2 and F3 C3 C3 C2 G2.
28 See my article 'The Performing Pitch of William Byrd's Latin Liturgical Polyphony', 102–4.
29 It is puzzling that the topmost parts of the first two 1588 items in the F4–C1 combination (nos 1–2) are also labelled 'triplex'. This may be an (admittedly obscure) direction to perform these items at the same pitch as the items in the F4–G2 combination; alternatively, it may be an error, which would at least explain why these and the subsequent 'triplex' designations were removed from later printings of the songbook.
30 The numbering is that assigned in Augustus Hughes-Hughes, *Catalogue of Manuscript Music in the British Museum*, vol. 3 (London: Trustees of the British Museum, 1909), 63–4. It excludes items from folios now missing but cited in the contemporary index, which is in the hand of the main scribe. A full inventory, including the missing items, will be found in Brett, 'Pitch and Transposition', 105–110.
31 See n. 30 above.
32 To explain these five exceptions, Brett posited that the arrangements had been made from transposed concordances cleffed F3–G2 ('Pitch and Transposition', 95). But his explanation cannot apply to two of the items in question (nos 12–13), which are church anthems and as such would only have been cleffed F4–C1.
33 There are no concordances for the missing original topmost solo voice parts of PL nos 35 ('My freedom, ah', BE15/21) and 36 ('What steps of strife', BE15/27).
34 See n. 30 above.

Ex. 2. Tablature, transcription and reconstructed score of 'What wights are these?'

no. 42) appears earlier in the same layer, where it is placed fifth in a series of eleven metrical psalms (nos 38–48), between two other items with flat signatures, and directly following two items whose strophes likewise culminate in vocal choruses.

For the same reasons that PL nos 76 and 78 are clearly arrangements for lute in G (see p. v above), so too is **6** (PL no. 80). Its chorus component may explain its placement immediately before 'Sith that the tree' (BE15/23), of which the *secunda pars*, preserved in PL only, appears to have been in partsong format. The internal indications that **8** (PL no. 78) was scored with two solo vocal parts (see p. x below) are corroborated by its placement between two consort duets, 'Delight is dead' (BE15/30) and 'Christ rising' (1589/46–7), and in a layer of PL containing no instrumental descants.

Method of Reconstructing Instrumental and Vocal Parts
As we have now seen, many essential musical parameters not explicit in the tablature—cleffing, notated pitch, and vocal-instrumental format—may be inferred from the surviving original versions of adjacent items in PL. Two parameters have nonetheless been lost—for the most part irretrievably—in the intabulation process: the assigning of notes to instrumental or vocal parts, and the individual durations of the vast majority of the notes themselves. A glance at the lute parts in exx. 2 and 3 will show that the adaptation of polyphony for performance on a non-sustaining instrument leaves us with the harmony without the counterpoint, the vertical without the horizontal, the weft without the warp.

A note-for-note, non-polyphonic transcription of the tablature has been included in each reconstructed score. Quasi polyphonic short-score transcriptions of the kind printed by Fellowes and Brett were deemed potentially prejudicial to the formation of a full score, less likely to reveal transcription errors, and insufficiently accountable to the source material. The tablature of items cleffed F3–G2 was transcribed initially as if for lute in A so the scores could be reconstructed untransposed in their original clefs (as shown by the vocal part of ex. 3). For practical purposes, these items were then transposed down a fourth to their presumed performing pitch, the transcribed tablature being transposed for lute in E.

In certain passages, the linearity of Byrd's original parts remains perfectly clear from the tablature. An example is the opening of 'What wights are these?' (**3**, shown in ex. 2), where, unusually for Byrd, the instruments enter in sequence from lowest to highest—V IV III I—and remain stratified in that order until after the vocal part has entered. In consequence, the extraction of II–V from the tablature begins as nothing more than a join-the-dots exercise. Though the *fuga* proceeds with great flexibility, even by Byrd's standards, the subject's up-down-up shape is distinct enough to reveal that II momentarily crosses below III in b. 7.

Considerable difficulties were encountered from the last minim of b. 8, however, whence the topmost notes of the tablature were at first mistaken for the vocal part. Only after much drafting and a trial performance was it realised that here II must again have crossed below III. A further problem was posed by the movement from the fourth minim of b. 10 to the beginning of b. 11. Here, to avoid direct octaves with V, Byrd's inner parts must have crossed, but the passage could not satisfactorily be reconstructed until it was recognised that the c' belonged to III, not IV, and that III first crossed below IV before crossing back again to the f'. Such crossing is of course normative in the inner parts of Byrd's consort songs, and its working out proves more laborious than any other aspect of the reconstructor's task.

Reconstruction of the instrumental descant involves (a) incorporating as much fugal activity as possible, (b) supplying imperfect consonance wherever it appears to be missing from the four intabulated parts, and (c) maintaining the general rhythmic density. The Spanish rubric indicates where, but not when, the descant enters; fortunately in bb. 1–4 the missing material is clearly mapped out by IV, a bar in advance and an octave lower. At b. 6, the crotchets in IV invite similar motion at the tenth above, but the temptation precisely to duplicate IV's rhythm had to be resisted in order to reserve I's share of the crotchet movement until bb. 7 and 10. In bb. 7–8, the tablature consists of perfect consonance only for two consecutive minims, suggesting that here I originally incorporated a 4–3 suspension. At b. 8, I joins the counter-exposition in which III, IV and V have already entered, being followed by II in b. 9.

In most cases the missing uppermost part is vocal as opposed to instrumental, and its reconstruction is considerably more straightforward. Not only does a verbal text serve as a guide in certain cases, but also, as Kerman observed,[35] the solo vocal part of any consort song by Byrd is highly stereotypical. It is almost invariably the last to enter,[36] it constantly echoes motives from the accompaniment, it is less rhythmically active than the accompanying parts, it keeps within a narrower range than the instruments,[37] and it moves predominantly by steps and small intervals. It repeats words only in particular circumstances, it is generally syllabic, reserving melismata for penultimate (or sometimes antepenultimate) syllables, and it invariably has a greater proportion of rests than the accompanying parts. To Kerman's list may be added the further observation that the solo vocal part terminates each line of the poem unmistakably on a cadence. It was chiefly this last characteristic that made it possible to deduce the metres of those of the present songs that lack their original verbal texts.

Most of these stereotypes are exemplified by the initial opening of **1**, where the original pentameter, if it were not already implicit in the song's AAB sonnet form, would still be perfectly clear from the positions of the cadences. As shown in ex. 3, the vocal part proceeds from the note indicated by the Spanish rubric and takes its next five notes directly from the *fuga* begun by the four accompanying parts (bb. 5–6). These six notes accommodate three iambic feet. The ensuing cadence (bb. 7–8) incorporates *basizans* (g–c) and *cantizans* (b–c') movement in the instrumental parts, but no *tenorizans* movement (the instrumental c' moves to e', not c'). Hence the vocal part must here have incorporated the *tenorizans* movement (d''–c''), accommodating another iambic foot. Between the three feet of the *fuga* and the one foot of the cadence there remains space for one further foot; its second note

---

35 *The Elizabethan Madrigal*, 103. Kerman's observations were made with the object of distinguishing adapted consort songs from original partsongs, but are no less useful to the reconstructor.
36 'Why do I use' (1588/33=BE16/26) is a noteworthy exception.

37 Though, as Kerman noted, the range of the solo vocal part is 'usually within an octave or a ninth', tenths and elevenths are not unknown (see, for example, 1588/4, 15, 23, 26 and 27; BE15/2, 7, 10, 15, 16, 17, 20, 29, 36, 37, 39, 40 and 41).

(*d''*) forms part of the *tenorizans* movement, leaving only its first note (*f''*) to be decided upon by melodic intuition and contrapuntal rule. Of the ten notes in the first line, therefore, only one cannot be extrapolated directly from the notes present in the tablature.

The melody of the remaining three lines of the quatrain may be reconstructed by the same method, intuition taking the place of motivicity as the latter decreases. The first four notes of the second line are clearly prefigured in thirds by the lowest two voices (bb. 8–9). The first four notes of the third line are much less obvious from the directly preceding interlude (bb. 12–13, where their rhythm is stretched and the second note is missing from the tablature) than they are from an echo in stretto (bb. 14–15). Missing imperfect consonances at all three cadences show the voice part to have incorporated in each case the *tenorizans* movement, the starkest of these indications being the bare semibreve towards the end of the second line (b. 11).

At any given moment in a song, the difficulty of reconstructing the parts, and the missing topmost part especially, depends largely on the extent to which Byrd's rhetorical purposes were served by *fuga*. Opening expositions, and the final couplets of **2** (b. 14f), **3** (b. 33f), **4** (b. 24f) and **5** (b. 25f), can be reconstructed with a good deal of confidence because they are intensely motivic and present the reconstructor with abundant clues. Each of the final couplets just referred to is the culmination of an ABABCC (or, in **3**, ABABBCC) scheme, and its heightened verbal rhyme is matched by heightened musical motivicity. Hence the more relaxed rhyme of the middle lines tends to be matched by a relaxation of the motivicity, rendering the parts much harder to reconstruct. The descant of **3**, for example, consists in bb. 18–21 and 24–6 almost entirely of guesswork, and it cannot be claimed to be definite, let alone definitive.

As we shall see, Paston's tablatures are demonstrably not entirely reliable, and the error quotient of the *unica* must be assumed to equal that of the other contents of PL. Yet since errors in the *unica* are by no means necessarily self-evident, it was decided that the reconstructions should follow the tablature as closely as possible. Only when a note or passage proved insoluble was the possibility of an error in the tablature entertained. Such an error is instantiated in ex. 2 by the first minim of b. 8, where various attempts to assign the *e'* to one of the inner parts came to nothing. It thus had to be concluded that the scribe, intending to notate the *a'* as a 2 for the *g'* course, at first wrote 2 erroneously for the *d'* course, and deemed it unnecessary to erase his error.

For all its endemic vagueness, the tablature is sometimes unexpectedly revealing. Though using different courses to represent two polyphonic parts can seldom have been practicable, this actually happens in b. 2 of ex. 2, where the two *d*'s are respectively assigned to the *a* and *d'* courses, and in b. 38 of **1**, where two notes in unison are sounded on different courses simultaneously. Even the seemingly egregious parallel motion occurring in b. 28 of **4** provides vital evidence of the arranger's method. In the first three minims of this bar, the general movement of the parts is clear enough to show incontrovertibly that, to obtain more practicable LH fingering, the A-minor chord has been redistributed. Other instances of chords with the same fingering were therefore checked in context, and were found to have been identically redistributed in two passages that would otherwise have remained perplexing (b. 41 of **4** and b. 7 of **8**).

Despite being misleading as to the original pitch of **5** (see p. v above), the song's lone surviving instrumental part from 423 proves surprisingly instructive as to the original disposition of the intabulated notes. To be able to refer to just one part considerably eases the reconstruction, particularly as regards the always challenging issue of part crossing. From b. 25, however, the 423 part becomes doubly informative. In Byrd's usual manner, the final couplet is sung twice, the repeat being fully written out in PL. On reaching b. 35, however, the 423 part does not repeat but instead proceeds differently, signalling an interchange of material with one of the other instruments. Hence in bb. 25–45, each ten-bar half of the 423 part supplies also the other ten-bar half of a second instrumental part, most probably in the same clef.

Was this illuminating interchange an aspect of Byrd's original conception, one of his own revisions, or the interference of a scribe? It is true that Byrd printed 'Though Amaryllis dance in green' (1588/12) with such an interchange, and that another occurs in his MS song 'While Phoebus used to dwell' (BE15/28). Yet these examples are isolated, the vast majority of repeats being merely signed rather than fully written out. Indeed, an interchange may not have taken place in certain copies of **5**, for at b. 35 PL transmits readings of the inner parts that differ from 423 at the very moment the repeat commences. That said, firmer evidence than this would be needed to controvert the interchange indicated by 423, and it seemed appropriate to incorporate similar interchanges in the written-out repeats of **1**, **2** and **4**. Even if those interchanges distort the composer's intentions, they arguably retain a double advantage of (a) making two of the instrumental parts as interesting as they possibly can be, and (b) maximising the chance that the material has been assigned to the correct instruments in *one* of the couplet's two iterations.

It is fortunate indeed that the most important of the PL *unica*—the through-composed consort song with chorus 'Look and bow down' (**8**)—happens also to be the most amenable to reconstruction. Not only does its verbal text survive in external sources (see below), but also the PL scribe greatly assisted the reconstructor's task by annotating the intabulation '6 voc.', and marking with a dot each fret number that belonged to a solo vocal part.[38] Brett established that the verbal text perfectly fitted the dotted vocal part in stanza one, and deemed the song to have been wholly a vocal duet in the manner of Byrd's consort anthem 'Christ rising' (1589/46–7), the following item in PL. He nonetheless admitted to having been 'unable to make a reconstruction along these lines'.[39]

Any such reconstruction would, in fact, be fatally flawed. It is clear from Byrd's only fully intact through-composed works for viols and voices—'Christ rising' and 'Have mercy upon me, O God' (1611/25)—that his practice was to leave one of the vocal parts tacet for whole sections. While both works, like 'Look and bow down', are in six parts, their chorus passages are scored mostly in five, so that in 'Christ rising' one of the duettists rests during choruses, while in 'Have mercy' one singer is assigned to the solo passages and another to the topmost part of the choruses. Only in the final chorus of each *pars* of 'Christ rising', and in

---

38 On the use of such dots to indicate a vocal line in vihuela tablature, see McCoy, 'Edward Paston and the Textless Lute-Song', 226.

39 BE16, 197.

Ex. 3. Tablature, transcription and reconstructed vocal part of 'Ah, youthful years'

the final chorus of 'Have mercy', are all six singers deployed simultaneously.[40]

The adjacent items in PL show that 'Look and bow down' must have incorporated a second solo vocal part in addition to the one indicated by the dots. Yet this cannot have been the case in stanza one, where the five intabulated parts are harmonically and contrapuntally self-sufficient, and prove quite incapable of having a sixth part added to them. It was not until stanza two, where only four parts are intabulated and none of them is marked with dots, that the missing uppermost part entered (and on the very note indicated by the Spanish rubric), leaving tacet the soloist from stanza one. At stanza three, however, where the PL scribe tellingly reiterated the annotation '6 voc.', the five intabulated parts are harmonically and contrapuntally insufficient, indicating beyond doubt that the texture incorporated a sixth part. And here the music can indeed be reconstructed as the duet Brett intuited.

The Poetry

The arrangements in PL are untexted, being identified only by brief verbal incipits entered by the principal scribe in the index and at the head of each item. In the case of 'Depart, ye furies' (**6**), the second and third words are supplied in the index alone. The incipits of three of the present eight songs are associable with complete verbal texts transmitted in other sources. 'I will give laud' (**7**) is readily identifiable as Thomas Sternhold's version of Psalm 34, which Byrd presumably drew directly from the English metrical psalter. The two other such texts survive in versions that clearly differ from those in which Byrd set them. 'In tower most high' (**2**) is doubtless a pre-publication version of Whitney's Diogenic emblem 'In crystal towers' (which Byrd went on to set as a three-voice partsong, 1611/8),[41] while 'Look and bow down' (**8**) has long been known from two divergent sources (see pp. xvi–xvii below), both of which ascribe the poem to Queen Elizabeth I and date it to the period of hubris following the Armada crisis of 1588.

Scholars have concurred that 'Look and bow down' is the queen's own work, and—on the basis of intimations in a contemporary ballad—that it was sung, in her presence and to Byrd's music, in St Paul's churchyard during the Armada state thanksgiving of 24 November.[42] It is of course conceded that such a performance, in the open air, would have required wind instruments; indeed, given that the churchyard was a noted site for congregational psalm singing,[43] the poem might more readily have been sung there to Luther's tune for the Lord's prayer (the only tune of requisite metre in the English psalter), Byrd's consort song being reserved for performance at court.

Wherever they were first sung, and to whatever music, these words seem rife with intimations that Elizabeth penned them expressly for Byrd to set. In a poem celebrating the failure of an invasion by the forces of the Counter-Reformation, it is surely surprising to find not only an equation of Elizabeth with the Blessed Virgin Mary but also outright mentions of priests, incense and sacrifice. Yet this fourfold red rag to Calvinist and Puritan readers appears also as the open expression of two private yet well-known circumstances: the queen's proclivity for religious ritual, and the trenchant Catholicism of her favourite composer. Her poetry (if hers it is), and his willingness to set it to music, could mean only that in the minds of both parties the separation of temporal and spiritual loyalties was absolute.

Thanks to PL's having been inventoried in an exhaustive survey of the sources of Elizabethan verse,[44] it has been firmly established that the five remaining present items have no known verbal concordances. This is by no means unusual in the songs of Byrd, whose printed collections contain settings of much poetry that is otherwise unknown. Yet it imposes the need for substitute texts, a need it would be impossible to meet were it not that the music of a strophic consort song, having to serve for two or more different verses, is more or less disallied from any one verse in particular. Even the single-verse elegy 'What wights are these?' (**3**), whose closing trumpet-calls may well originally have served as an audible metaphor for the Last Judgement, seems by and large to have maintained the customary polite distance between words and music. 'A general correspondence,' wrote Brett, 'is usually all that exists between voice and verse: little else, one feels, would prevent the exchange between songs of poems sharing the same metrical and stanzaic form.'[45]

With or without Byrd's approval, contemporary practice did not scruple to match existing consort songs with new or borrowed words. We learn from the epistle dedicatory of *The paradyse of daynty deuises* that the anthology's contents are 'aptly made to be set to any song in five parts, or song to instrument[s]'.[46] While it cannot be proved that this incitement led directly to any of the surviving settings of poems from *The paradyse*,[47] three of Byrd's songs exist with what are demonstrably substitute texts by Paston.[48] A further such text may well have been written by him for a fourth song, copied by Robert Dow with the words 'Blame I confess' (BE15/15), which in PL and other Paston MSS appears with the incipit 'Remember Lord'. Nor, therefore, can the other verbal *unica* in PL be held entirely above suspicion of representing different texts from those originally set by the composer.

The liberties taken by Paston furnished a historical precedent for the modern editing of 'My freedom, ah' (BE15/21), of which only the four accompanying viol parts with their verbal incipit survive. For his reconstruction of the voice part, Fellowes for some reason chose Whitney's pentameter verse 'In crystal towers' (mentioned above), even though it could be fitted to the music only by dint of truncating certain lines. This unfortunate situa-

---

40 In its pre-publication version, the final chorus of the *secunda pars* of 'Christ rising' was scored for only five voices, the sixth voice joining in the 'Amen': see BE11/13.

41 Similarly, Byrd set 'Susanna fair' both as a consort song (1588/29) and as a three-voice partsong (1589/8).

42 See Brett's remarks in BE 16, 197–8; see also Arthur F. Marotti and Steven W. May, 'Two Lost Ballads of the Armada Thanksgiving Celebration', *English Literary Renaissance*, 41 (2011), 31–63 (46–50).

43 Peter le Huray, *Music and the Reformation in England, 1549–1660* (London: Herbert Jenkins, 1967; repr. Cambridge: Cambridge University Press, 1978), 375.

44 Steven W. May and William A. Ringler Jr, *Elizabethan Poetry: A Bibliography and First-Line Index of English Verse, 1559–1603*, 3 vols (London: Thoemmes Continuum, 2004). Records from this publication are searchable via the *Union First Line Index of English Verse* (<firstlines.folger.edu>).

45 BE15, p. vi.

46 London: Henry Disle, 1576; STC 7516 and later edns, sig. A2v.

47 See *Consort Songs*, ed. Philip Brett, MUSICA BRITANNICA, vol. 22 (London: Stainer & Bell, 1967), nos 17–23.

48 1589/31, BE15/28 and 31; see Philip Taylor, 'Music and Recusant Culture: The Paston Manuscript Collection and William Byrd's Songs' (PhD diss., University of Lancaster, 2007), 144–61.

tion was remedied by Brett, who substituted instead the mixed hexameter and tetrameter text of another of Byrd's songs, 'I thought that love had been a boy' (1589/32). The substitution is justifiable not only on the grounds of being a good fit, but also because 'My freedom, ah' is found only in MSS from Paston's collection and thus not inconceivably represents another of his adaptations.

The same justifications will, it is hoped, be conceded to the three present reconstructions with texts purloined from Tudor publications. Admittedly, had Byrd actually set the text of 'Lo, dead he lives' he would doubtless have repeated its initial vocative 'Lo' (as, for example, in the repetition of 'Look' at the beginning of **8**). In all other respects, however, the substitute poem's elegiac mood and unusual seven-line structure seem well suited to the music of 'What wights are these?' (**3**). Whitney's 'Narcissus lov'd' is one of a host of poems in Venus and Adonis stanzas that might practicably be sung to the music of 'With sighs and tears' (**4**), although this particular association of words and music seems in a minute way corroborated by the fortuitous mirror image formed in b. 10 by the instrumental bass and the reconstructed voice part. In contrast, the compatibility of Lord Thomas Vaux's 'What grieves my bones?' with the music of 'O happy thrice' (**5**) may be more than mere chance. Apparently, the lost original song text not only borrowed its first three words from Vaux's last line, but also (as far as may be judged from the reconstructed vocal part) assimilated his verse structure in close detail, as if penned as an answer-poem or 'reply'.

In terms of prosody, verbal repetition and melismata, the reconstructed vocal parts of the two remaining songs proved so exacting that it seemed highly unlikely their requirements could be satisfied by any substitute Tudor texts. Instead, their verbal incipits from PL have been taken up by Nicholas Williams as starting points for pastiche lyrics, following the precedent of Brett's ingenious continuation of the text of 'Where the blind' (BE15/39). 'Ah, youthful years' (**1**), readily identified by its AAB structure as one of Byrd's sonnet settings,[49] calls *inter alia* for a calculated choice of unstressed syllables for the melismata of its final couplet (see b. 60f; the words 'despite' and 'delight' occur with melismatic first syllables elsewhere in Byrd's songs). In the case of 'Depart, ye furies' (**6**), whose verbal incipit cites the stage topoi encountered in *Gorboduc* and later English tragedies, certain metrical irregularities implied by the music seem most likely the symptoms of a dramatic as opposed to a poetic text. In a notable departure from Byrd's customary strophic forms, the opening (apparently prose) lines receive their own separate setting before the music settles into regular repeating stanzas. With neither an intact verbal text nor a corollary in the composer's output, the reconstruction of this song remains the most conjectural of all.

The Authority and Use of the Reconstructions
The present reconstructions do not and cannot precisely represent Byrd's original scores. This is a matter not merely of assumption but of scientific fact. On surveying a sample of sixteen items from PL with concordances in Byrd's prints, Sequera found their tablatures to correspond to the prints within an accuracy range of 88.9 to 96.7 per cent, the average accuracy being 92.4 per cent.[50] For the reasons given above, however, the reconstructions have followed the tablatures as closely as possible, resulting in a correspondence well above the statistical average. In the case of **1**, for example, twenty-two notes of the reconstructed score differ from the 893 comprised by the intabulation, yielding a correspondence of 97.5 per cent. If this intabulation is assumed to have been of average accuracy, then more than five per cent of the reconstructed instrumental matter must consist of undetected errors. To that percentage must of course be added further, unquantifiable margins of error regarding (a) the allocation of notes to parts, and (b) the reconstructed vocal part, which especially in the three lines preceding the final couplet still awaits an unexceptionable solution.

In the epistle dedicatory of his 1588 songbook, Byrd registered his concern (albeit in a form of the modesty topos) about 'many untrue incorrected copies of divers my songs spread abroad'. Nearly four hundred years later, in his discussion of 'Look and bow down', Brett concluded that a reconstruction would be 'necessarily so tentative as to make it unworthy of the composer and possibly misleading about his intentions'.[51] These points of view bear the utmost authorial and scholarly weight, and resonate as stern warnings against all attempts of the kind made here.

Any reconstruction, however, must be evaluated on its own terms: as a reconstruction *per se* and not as a resurrection. While much has inevitably been lost in translation as the songs have passed from staff notation to tablature and back again, each has powerfully—no less powerfully, perhaps, than any of Byrd's intact songs—retained a character all of its own. This suggests, given the undeniable inaccuracies of melody and scoring, that a good deal of each song's uniqueness resides in the factor best preserved in the intabulation process, and a factor about which we still have much to learn from Byrd's music: the contrasts and timings of its harmony.

With the possible exception of **8**, which is of much interest extra-musically, performers should concentrate on Byrd's intact songs, and on those songs reconstructed by Brett, before giving consideration to the present reconstructions. These do not form a set, and they must not be performed as such, but individually some may prove useful as adjuncts to cognate songs. Inevitably, performing the reconstructed songs alongside intact ones will expose weaknesses in the former, but if that leads to further, more convincing attempts at reconstruction, and/or to the identifying or composition of different substitute poetry for **1** and **3–6**, then my efforts will have served a useful purpose.

An authentic rationale for programming these reconstructions is provided by the fastidious organisation of PL. Nos 14–19 form a sequence of songs with written final C, any three or more of which would make up a logical performing set (it goes without

---

49 Other AAB sonnet settings are 1588/18 and 20 and 1589/15–16, 17–18, 26 and 36–7.
50 These figures were kindly supplied by Dr Sequera, and have here been rounded to one decimal place.
51 BE16, p. 197.

saying that, in line with the reconstructions, the intact songs must be transposed a fourth lower):
- 'Ah, youthful years' (**1**)
- 'As I beheld, I saw a herdman wild' (1588/20)
- 'Who likes to love' (1588/13)
- 'In tower most high' (**2**)
- 'Though Amarillis dance in green' (1588/12)
- 'What grieves my bones?' (**5**)

Nos 29–31 form a triptych with written final A:
- 'As Caesar wept' (BE15/14)
- 'Narcissus lov'd' (**4**)
- 'Susanna fair' (1588/29)

Nos 40–42 form a sequence of three psalms with vocal chorus:
- 'O Lord, who in thy sacred tent' (1588/6=BE16/8)
- 'The man is blest' (BE15/4)
- 'I will give laud' (**7**)

Three further psalms with vocal choruses which may be performed alongside the above are 'O Lord, within thy tabernacle' (BE15/1, not in PL), 'The Lord is only my support' (BE15/2, PL no. 44) and 'Lord, to thee I make my moan' (BE15/5, PL no. 47).

Nos 51–2 form a pair of sad songs with final D:
- 'If that a sinner's sighs' (1588/30=BE16/23)
- 'Lo, dead he lives' (**4**)

Use might also be made of **4** in a selection of Byrd's elegies (1588/34–5, BE15/29–32).

The forces required by 'Look and bow down' (**8**) are those required also for four consort anthems by Byrd:
- 'Christ rising' (1589/46–7)
- 'Have mercy upon me, O God' (1611/25)
- 'Hear my prayer, O Lord' (BE11/14)*
- 'O Lord, rebuke me not' (BE11/15)*

Though 'Depart, ye furies' (**6**) likewise requires a vocal chorus, its pagan ethos and inferred original function ally it instead with Byrd's small but significant corpus of dramatic songs:
- 'Blame I confess' (BE15/15)
- 'Delight is dead' (BE15/30)
- 'If trickling tears' (BE16/39)*
- 'Penelope that longed' (1588/27)
- 'Quis me statim' (BE15/37)
- 'Wretched Albinus' (BE15/41)

A Note on Performing Pitch

We await the discovery of evidence directly bearing on the performing pitch of English pre-Restoration secular music. Given, however, that consort songs were written for performance by choristers, it may well be significant that in his solo vocal parts Byrd generally observed an uppermost limit of d'' (or g'', its equivalent in F3–G2 clefs), for this is precisely the uppermost limit observed also in the services and anthems those choristers sang in cathedral or chapel. This naturally suggests performance of the songs a semitone higher than concert pitch (i.e. at $a' = 466.2$ Hz), the nearest practical modern equivalent of the historic quire pitch determinable from seventeenth-century organ pipes ($a' = c.\ 475$ Hz).[52]

Acknowledgements

My thanks are due to many individuals who have contributed to the preparation of this collection in ways great and small, and to four collaborators in particular. As PI of the AHRC-funded Tudor Partbooks project, Prof. Magnus Williamson convened an invaluable series of public reconstruction workshops in 2015 and 2016, during which group study of PL tablatures led to the first drafts of **5** and **7**, and the first trial performances were given of **7** and **8**. Dr Hector Sequera has generously shared his unrivalled knowledge of the vihuela tradition and the Paston lutebooks, and facilitated trial performances of **2** and **3** that prompted essential revisions to both reconstructions. Prof. Nicholas Williams, in addition to providing indispensable substitute texts for **1** and **6**, supplied a series of draft texts in various metres for **3** until the reconstructed music became focussed enough to reveal its compatibility with an historic text. Time and again, Prof. Williams willingly sacrificed his better poetic instincts to my stringent (and repeatedly misguided) musical demands. Above all, my thanks are due to Bill Hunt for facilitating the performance, recording and publication of these and others of my reconstructions, which without his encouragement would never have seen the light of day. It remains only to say that the blame is mine alone for every error that reconstruction has added to these precious fragments of Byrd's art.

Andrew Johnstone
Dublin, December 2020

---

* Reconstruction to be published separately.
52 See my article '"As it was in the beginning": Organ and Choir Pitch in Early Anglican Church Music', *Early Music*, 31 (2003), 506–525.

EDITORIAL METHOD

The lute tablature (tab.) has been transcribed into staff notation not for performance purposes but as a ready means of representing the source material. To facilitate collation with PL (for images of this important MS see <www.bl.uk/manuscripts/>), the lute parts are annotated with the relevant folio numbers, each line break in the tab. being indicated with a pilcrow (¶).

Accidentals, both in the transcriptions of the tab. and in the instrumental and vocal parts, are applicable according to modern usage. In the textual commentary below, chords quoted from the tab. are given as fret numbers ordered from the lowest- to the highest-sounding course, unused courses being represented by dots. Hence on a lute tuned $G\ c\ f\ a\ d'\ g'$, the chord $A\ f\ c\ f'$ is quoted as 2·033·.

In BE, viol parts reconstituted from lute and keyboard arrangements are printed in small type (see, for example, BE15/25). To observe that policy in the present collection, however, would leave only the quintus part of **5** in regular type; hence small type has been reserved for notes not present in the tab. (including in all cases the uppermost part in the score) and for sharps, naturals and flats that differ from the tab. (all of which are explained in the commentary). Excepting the quintus part just mentioned, and the material derived directly from it, the time value of every note longer than its equivalent in the tab. is editorial, as too is the assigning of notes to parts.

As a rule, the arranger of the tab. appears to have substituted two repeated semibreves for an original breve, and two repeated minims for an original syncopated semibreve comprising the preparation and dissonance of a suspension. Such repeated notes have been amalgamated without comment.

Notes exceeding the lowest limit of the lute and transposed an octave higher by the arranger (see, for example, **8** bb. 39–40) have been restored to their presumed original octave, also without comment. All other differences between the reconstructed score and the tab. are signalled by parenthetical numbers below the lute part and are explicated in the commentary.

Notes that are presumed to have been present in the original parts comprehended by the tab. but are missing from it are classified in the commentary as either *excised* (when the arranger appears to have omitted them deliberately to simplify the fingering) or *lacunary* (when they appears to have been omitted in error).

Part-names are editorial. In Byrd's publications and in contemporary English domestic manuscripts, the naming of inner and uppermost parts follows no common pattern. For consistency within the present collection, the solo vocal part is named *cantus*, the instrumental part immediately below it is named *altus*, the lowest two parts are named *tenor* and *bassus* respectively, the remaining instrumental part *quintus* and the second solo vocal part (in **8**) *sextus*. In the commentary, vocal and instrumental parts are identified by the ordinal numbers of their respective staves in capital roman numerals, staves being numbered from the top down.

Nos 1–5 incorporate repeats of verses or couplets that are fully written out in the tab.. In these repeats, the two iterations are never identical, and a reading given in one iteration may be preferable to that given in the other. Readings rejected on these grounds are reported with the phrase 'substituted with', the preferred reading being identified by bar number, decimal point and chord number(s) ('23.5–6', for example, means 'the fifth and sixth chords of bar 23 of the tab.').

Except in citations of printed sources and in the textual study of the words of **8** (p. xvi–xvii below), spelling has been modernised without comment.

TEXTUAL COMMENTARY

1 Ah, youthful years
music: PL ff. 9v–10r
La p[rimera] all 3. t[raste] = first course, third fret
bb. 41–4: the vocal part resembles 1588/4 bb. 25–6 and BE15/13 bb. 3–5

(1) substituted with 26.2
(2) *A* added to IV to complete the motive taken up by the voice part in b. 13 (that this note should be lacunary is surprising given that it would be sounded on an open course)
(3) substituted with 7.4
(4) as (2) above
(5) substituted with 19.1
(6) *e* in tab. possibly an error for *e'*
(7) *b* presumed excised to simplify ·2053· to ·20·3·
(8) *f*-sharp presumed excised from tab. to simplify ·5433· to ··033·
(9) *e* in tab. substituted with *a* in IV to allow consonant 6-5 movement in voice part
(10) *b* presumed lacunary
(11) *B* in tab. assumed to represent the doubled *b* in II and III
(12) the implication of minim cut-offs and an abrupt harmonic shift suggests an error in the tab.
(13) if the notes clearly missing from the tab. at this point have been inferred correctly, then a complete tab. would have been the awkward 2·20·2; the missing notes cannot confidently be deemed either excised or lacunary, their absence seeming rather to imply indecision on the arranger's part as to what, and what not, might best be excised
(14) *d* in IV by analogy with voice part in b. 56
(15) *b* presumed lacunary

(16)   substituted with 72.3
(17)   substituted with 75.2
(18)   substituted with 64.1
words: specially written by N. J. A. Williams

2 In tower most high
music: PL ff. 11v–12r
La s[egun]^da all 3. t[raste] = second course, third fret
(1)   erroneous a'-sharp results from the fourth fret's having been indicated mistakenly on the f-sharp course instead of the d-course
(2)   since a literal reading of the tab. would incorporate direct octaves with the reconstructed voice part at this point, and there is no compelling reason for reconstructing the voice part any differently, the c' in the tab. is assumed to result from the first fret's having been indicated mistakenly on the b course instead of the f-sharp course, similarly to (1) above
(3)   substituted with 21.1
(4)   rhythm inferred from barring in tablature
(5)   substituted with 25.1
(6)   substituted with 25.5
(7)   rhythm inferred from barring in tab.
(8)   substituted with 15.2
(9)   rhythm inferred from barring in tab.
(10) d presumed lacunary

words: by Geoffrey Whitney, printed with a dedication to Edward Paston in *CE*, 198–9. The verbal incipit given in PL, 'In tower most high', has been retained, Whitney's published incipit 'In crystal towers' being incompatible with Byrd's opening motive. That the present song was a setting of a pre-publication version of the poem is suggested not only by the two readings of the incipit but also by the composer's subsequent decision to set v. 1 of the published version completely anew as a three-voice partsong (1611/8). At bars 9–10, two versions of the reconstructed voice part have had to be supplied because the verbal repetition implicit in Byrd's music involves seven syllables in vv. 1, 2 and 5 but only six in vv. 3 and 4. Such an expedient would be exceptional for Byrd, but may well have been unnecessary for the pre-publication version of the poem.

Vv. 1, 3 and 5 form a self-contained narrative and may be performed as such; vv. 2 and 4 refer to the Cynic philosopher Diogenes, and may be inserted if desired:

> 2. Diogenes within a tun did dwell,
>   No choice of place, nor store of pelf he had;
> And all his goods could Bias bear right well,
>   And Codrus had small cates, his heart to glad:
>   His meat was roots: his table was a stool,
>   Yet these for wit did set the world to school?

> 4. What man is rich? not he that doth abound;
>   What man is poor? not he that hath no store:
> But he is rich that makes content his ground;
>   And he is poor that covets more and more.
>   Which proves the man was richer in the tun
>   Than was the king that many lands had won.

3 Lo, dead he lives *to the music of* What wights are these?
music: PL f. 28v
La p[rimera] al 2. t[raste] = first course, second fret
b. 23: close octaves of the kind occurring here between I and IV are by no means unknown in Byrd's songs (see, for example, BE15/24 bb. 17–18, BE16/20 bb. 25–6, BE16/27 b. 9)
bb. 27–37: the repeat is fully written out in the tablature, the only difference being that on the first iteration at bar 34 the first two crotchets are substituted with a minim chord $\cdot\cdot 0\cdot 32 = ff\ a$ (edn follows second iteration)
(1)   apparently the LH fingering 2···2 was at first written 2···2· and the error left uncorrected
(2)   rhythm inferred from barring in tab.
(3)   this note perhaps accommodated a hypersyllable in the original words
(4)   the tab. implies direct fifths and is inimical to a fifth part, implying that d' and f' were respectively substituted for g' and a' to simplify the LH fingering from ··2153 ·54·75 to ··2103 ·54·35
(5)   apparently the original III was transposed an octave lower, and the original IV omitted, to simplify ····53 ··0375 to ···1·0 ··0035
(6)   substituted with 42.2

(7) substituted with 38.3
(8) substituted with 39.1
words: anonymous, 'Of the death of Sir Thomas Wyatt the Elder' (TM, f. 89r)

4 Narcissus lov'd *to the music of* **With sighs and tears**
music: PL ff. 17v–18r
La p[rimera] vasio = first course, open
b. 24f: the point introduced here is found in several other compositions by Byrd (see 1588/1 bb. 45–7, 1591/19 b. 62f, BE9/13 b. 68f, BE15/19 b. 14f, BE15/21 b. 18f)
(1) minims followed by a crotchet at the same pitch were most likely tied here (compare the similar counterpoint at bb. 46–7 of **8**)
(2) b' added editorially to complete motive in III
(3) f-sharp (open course) in tab. possibly an error for b (open course)
(4) rhythm of II is unidiomatic in tab. and has been substituted with a rhythm more characteristic of the composer
(5) c in IV presumably transposed an octave higher in tab. to simplify 5323·· to 0231· (compare 36.3 and 41.1 below)
(6) substituted with 39.3–4
(7) tab. includes at least one note too many: substituted with 40.1
(8) g'-natural preferred, to match 24.3 and avoid melodic diminished 4th in III
(9) substituted with 25.4–5
(10) substituted with 26.1
(11) c in IV presumably omitted from tab. to simplify 5323·· to ·023··
(12) as (5) above
words: Geoffrey Whitney (*CE*, 149)

5 What grieves my bones? *to the music of* **O happy thrice**
music: PL f. 12v; 423 p. 52 (III only, 'contratenor', a tone lower)
La p[rimera] al 3. t[raste] = first course, third fret
bb. 25–35 of IV are derived from bb. 35–45 of III, and bars 35–45 of IV are derived from bb. 25–35 of III, the two parts clearly having interchanged material on the repeat of the final couplet
(1) b in III presumably substituted with d in tab. to simplify ·2·53· to ·20·3·
(2) variant readings (edn follows 423)
(3) either variant readings (edn follows 423) or b in III substituted with g in tab. to simplify 2043·· to 2013··
(4) g' of III transposed down an octave to simplify 3··887 to 3·5·37
(5) the layout of the tab. suggests that at this point III and IV did not cross and subsequently exchange material in the exemplars from which PL derives
(6) g' of IV transposed as (4) above
words: Lord Thomas Vaux, 'In his extreme sickness' (*PDD*, 3), to which the original text may have been an answer-poem (see preface)

6 Depart, ye furies
music: PL f. 47r
La p[rimera] vasio = first course, open
b. 22: on the close octaves between I and IV, see the note to b. 23 of **3** above
(1) f-sharp by analogy with 3.4
(2) general rest indicated by vertical row of dots in tab.
(3) dotted minim chord indicated by vertical row of dots in tab.
(4) as (3) above
(5) notes of III presumed lacunary
(6) notes of II presumed lacunary
(7) notes of IV presumed lacunary
words: specially written by N. J. A. Williams

7 I will give laud
music: PL f. 23v
La s[egun]^{da} all 3. t[raste] = second course, third fret
(1) f' presumed an error for f
(2) g' and c' presumed lacunary
(3) general rest indicated by vertical row of dots in tab.
(4) d in tab. presumed to represent the doubled d' in II and III
(5) presumed original e-flat substituted with c' in tab. to simplify 53·· 10 to ·0·310
(6) as (3) above
(7) b'-flat in II presumed lacunary
(8) c in tab. ·0···· presumed an error for a ···0··
(9) d in tab. ·2···· presumed an error for g ··2···
(10) f presumed lacunary
(11) a presumed excised from tab. to simplify ·5433· to ··033·
(12) f presumed lacunary
words: Ps. 34, vv. 1–10, versified by Thomas Sternhold (S&H)

8 Look and bow down
music: PL ff. 43v–44v
La p[rimera] vasio = first course, open (i.e. the first vocal note of the second stanza)
bb. 7–11: the monotony in III is closely matched in BE15/12 bb. 6–9
b. 12 (II and IV) and bb. 71–3 (I and V): on the close octaves between these pairs of voices, see the note to b. 23 of **3** above
(1) d' presumed an error for d
(2) e-flats presumably transposed an octave higher in tab. to simplify 5323·· to ·0231·
(3) f-natural by analogy with 11.1
(4) c presumably excised from tab to simplify 53·310 to ·3·310
(5) IV must be f-natural to reach the following b-flat grammatically
(6) general rest indicated by vertical row of dots in tab.
(7) b-flat (which inevitably causes direct octaves between II and V) presumably substituted in tab. for an original g to simplify ·32653 to ·35653
(8) g presumed lacunary
(9) d' in tab. presumed to represent the doubled d in V and VI
(10) all minims followed by a crotchet at the same pitch were most likely tied here (compare the similar counterpoint at bb. 6–7 of **4**)
(11) g' presumed an error for g
(12) d presumed lacunary
(13) b-flat presumed lacunary
(14) flat to e' presumably overlooked by arranger or missing from exemplar
(15) f, b-flat and d' are all assigned in tab. to the fifth fret, the f apparently in error
(16) notes of II presumed lacunary
(17) f presumed an error for f'
(18) d in tab. presumed to represent the doubled d' in III and IV
(19) d presumed lacunary
(20) g' in tab. implies a different division of II's sustained g' into shorter, repeated notes, but assigning a syllable to the following g' in the tab. yields a more satisfactory text underlay; c' presumably omitted from tab. to simplify 5323·0 to ·323·0 (compare 7.1 above)
(21) though present in tab., the e'-flat cannot be accommodated in the counterpoint
(22) G presumed lacunary
words: SNG/4, *CMC* sigs D6v–D7r
PL supplies verbal incipits for stanzas one and three; the latter, deemed 'garbled' by Brett, provides a third reading of line 13. The three verbal sources are transcribed below.

SNG/4
A songe made by her ma[jes]^tie and songe before her at her cominge from white hall to Powles throughe fleetestre[et] in Anno D[omi]ni 1588
[in margin] Songe in December after the scatteringe of the Spanishe Navy

1 Loke and bowe downe thyne eare O Lorde
2 from thy bright spheare behoulde and see
3 Thy hand maide and thy handy worke
4 Amongst thy pristes offeringe to thee
5 zeal for incense reachinge the skyes
6 my self and septer sacryfyce

7 my sowle assend his holy place
8 Ascribe him strenght and singe him prayse
9 for he restraynethe Pryinces ~~sprghts~~ spyrits
10 And hath done wonders in my daies
11 he made the wynds and waters rise
12 To scatter all myne enemyes

13 Tis Josephes Lorde and Israells god
14 the fyry pillar and dayes clowde
15 That saved his Sainctes from wicked men
16 And drenchet the honor of the prowde
17 And hath p^reserved in tender love
18 The Spirit of his Turtle dove

PL
1 Looke and bow downe
13 Tis Josephs hearde

CMC
The other song of Queene Elizabeth made in manner of a thanksgiving to God for her and our deliverance from the invincible Navie of the Spaniard (as he termed it) which thanks and praise was performed at Sainte Pauls crosse in London.

Looke and bow downe thine eare O Lord,
  from thy bright spheare behold and see
Thy handmaid and thy handy worke,
  among thy Priests offring to thee.
Ecco's resounding up the skies:
my selfe and scepter sacrifice,

My soule ascend his holy place,
  ascribe him strength, and sing him prayse:
For hee restraineth Princes spirits,
  and hath wrought wonders in our dayes.
He made the windes and waters rise:
  and did destroy mine enemies.

This Jacobs head, this Israels God,
  the fiery pillar and the cloud:
Which kept the saints from Pharaohs rod,
  and drencht the honour of the proud:
He hath preserved now in love,
  the soule of me his turtle dove.

Of the poem's two complete sources, neither can be given priority on obvious textual or circumstantial grounds. SNG/4, a single folio numbered 60, originally formed part of a commonplace book owned by the distinguished legal historian Sir Henry Spelman (1563/4–1641): see *Elizabeth I: Collected Works*, ed. Leah S. Marcus, Janel Mueller and Mary Beth Rose (Chicago and London: University of Chicago Press, 2000), p. 410. Though *CMC* postdates the Armada crisis by some fifty years, its claim to be an enlarged reprint of a volume first printed in 1588 (sigs A1r–A2v) is corroborated by an entry in the Stationers' Register for 12 December in that year, within three weeks of the state thanksgiving: see *A Transcript of the Registers of the Company of Stationers of London, 1554–1640*, ed. Edward Arber, vol. 2 (London: privately printed, 1875), p. 511. No copies of the 1588 printing survive, but if it included 'Look and bow down' then the *CMC* readings are presumably at only one remove from it. In *CMC* the poem is the second of two attributed to Elizabeth, the first being 'Deliver me O Lord my God' (sig. D6r–v; a recension of the text of John Bull's verse anthem 'Deliver me, O God').

Since neither SNG/4 nor *CMC* entirely fits the music, a conflation of the two is unavoidable. Both sources transmit lines 1–3, 6–9, 11 and 16 without disagreement, and lines 4 and 10 with only trivial differences. Substantive differences in lines 5, 12, 17 and 18 may be resolved by reference to Byrd's presumed word repetition ('To scatter, to scatter all mine enemies', bb 67–8) and melodic profiles ('the soul of *me*', bb. 117–24), or even to both ('zeal for incense, zeal for incense', bb. 21–5; 'he hath preserv-ed, he hath preserv-ed, bars 103–7). (To assume that this approach reveals the readings actually set by Byrd is tempting but unwise: as PL's incipit for line 13 shows, the version of the poem that circulated with his music incorporated one reading not transmitted by either of the intact versions, and might therefore have incorporated others.)

Given that it transmits the readings of lines 5 and 12 that are compatible with the music, SNG/4 has been followed entirely for stanzas one and two. But while *CMC* transmits the readings of lines 17 and 18 that are compatible with the music, it cannot be followed entirely for stanza three. To be sure, in line 15 *CMC*'s 'Pharaoh's rod' is more poetic than SNG/4's 'wicked men', but the fact of its being the only cross-rhyme in the poem marks it out as someone's idea of an improvement (the same might be said also of *CMC*'s 'wrought' in line 10). In line 13 (assuming *CMC*'s 'head' to be a corruption of PL's 'hearde'), two possible allusions to the book of Genesis are suggested by the intact versions: Jacob's cunning augmentation of his own livestock at the expense of his father-in-law Laban's (Gen.30:31–43) and the Lord's favour to the imprisoned Joseph in Egypt (Gen.39:22–3). There is little sense, however, either in PL's attribution of a herd to Joseph, or in *CMC*'s association of Jacob's herd with imagery from the book of Exodus. The simplest explanation for the three readings, then, is that first 'Josephes Lorde' was somehow corrupted to 'Josephs hearde', thence rationalised (in some lost intermediate source, and on the basis of Gen.30:31–43) to 'Jacobs hearde', and finally corrupted to 'Jacobs head'. These things considered, SNG/4 has been followed as far as line 16, and *CMC* for lines 17–18.

1. Ah, youthful years

words by
N. J. A. Williams

©2020 Fretwork Editions FE33: William Byrd, Eight Fragmentary Songs, edited and reconstructed by Andrew Johnstone

2. In tower most high

words by Geoffrey Whitney

3. Lo, dead he lives
to the music of What wights are these?

Words anon.
'Of the death of Sir Thomas Wyatt the elder'

©2020 Fretwork Editions FE33: William Byrd, Eight Fragmentary Songs, edited and reconstructed by Andrew Johnstone

on: Which shows, which shows self - love, from which there few can
see: And why? Be - cause self - love, self - love doth wound our
teem? Or can, or can we see so soon an - o - ther's

'scape, A plague too rife: be - witch - eth ma - ny a one.
hearts, And makes us think our deeds a - lone to be.
miss? And not our own? O blind - ness most ex - treme!

The rich, the poor, the learn - ed and the sot Of - fend there -
Which se - cret sore lies hid - den from our eyes, And yet the
Af - fect not then but try, and prove thy deeds, For of self -

5. What grieves my bones?
to the music of O happy thrice

words by Lord Thomas Vaux
'In his extreme sickness'

What grieves my bones, and makes my body faint?
I toss as one be-tossed in waves of care,
Then hold thee still, let be thy hea-vi-ness;

©2020 Fretwork Editions FE33: William Byrd, Eight Fragmentary Songs, edited and reconstructed by Andrew Johnstone

6. Depart, ye furies

Words by
N. J. A. Williams

©2020 Fretwork Editions FE33: William Byrd, Eight Fragmentary Songs, edited and reconstructed by Andrew Johnstone

*Though in the MS the repeat is signalled from 26.2, it seems much more likely that this material from bb. 23–5 was originally inserted between verses.

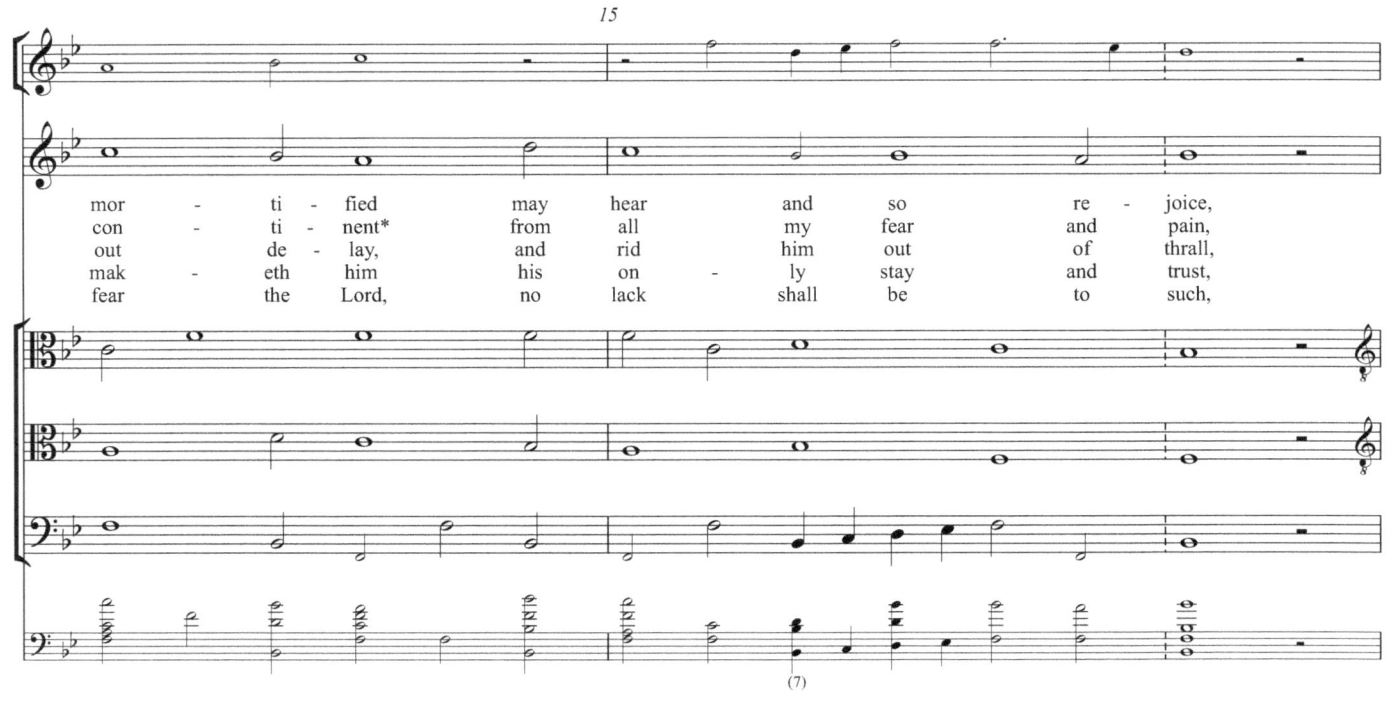

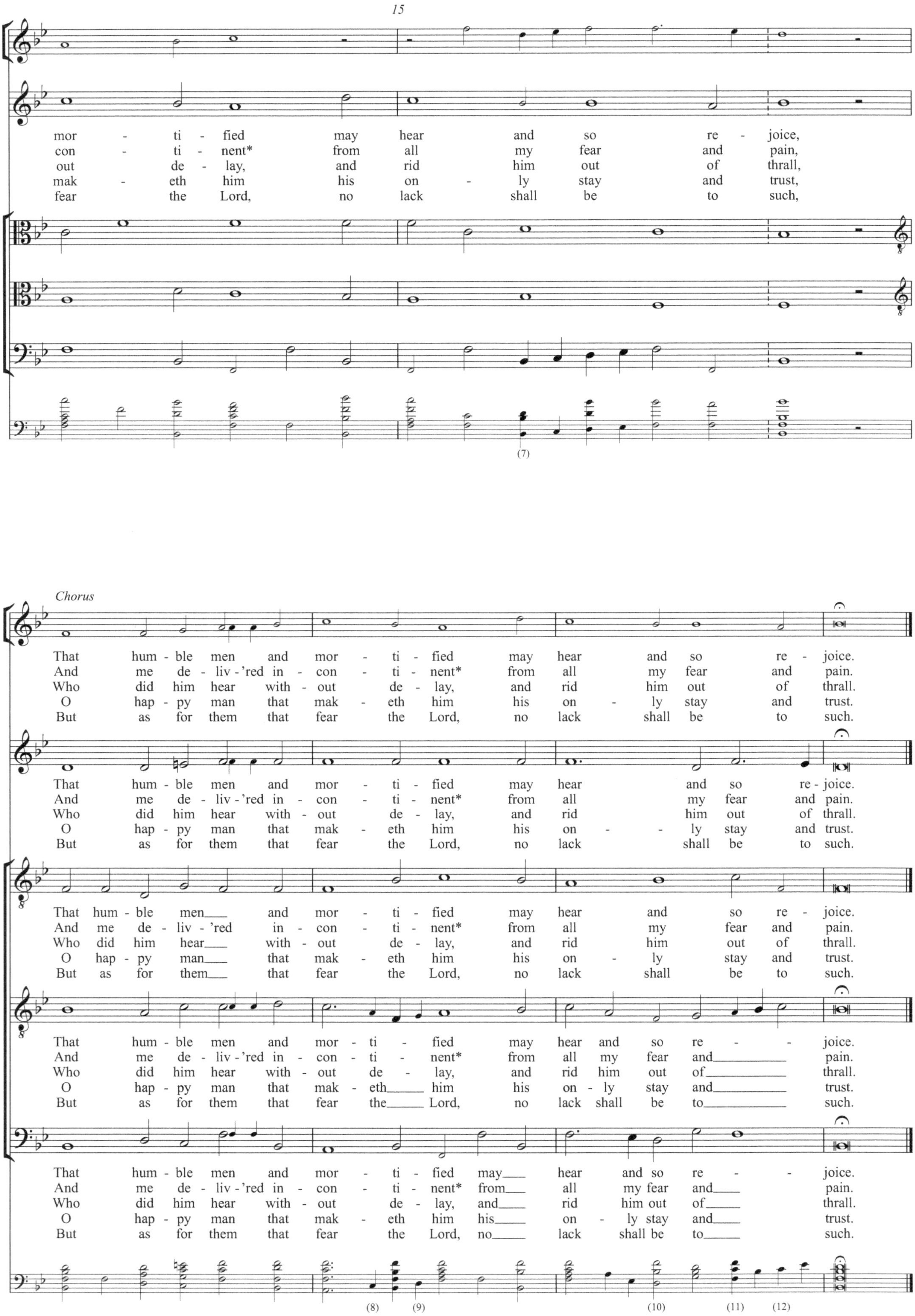

* i.e. without delay, immediately

8. Look and bow down

Words attrib.
Queen Elizabeth I

©2020 Fretwork Editions FE33: William Byrd, Eight Fragmentary Songs, edited and reconstructed by Andrew Johnstone

www.ingramcontent.com/pod-product-compliance
Lightning Source LLC
Chambersburg PA
CBHW042017090526
44588CB00024B/2892